The Fascinating Fibonaccis

"Coloured Bedtime StoryBook"

By

Shonali Chinniah

Illustrated by

Hari Kumar Nair

ILLUSTRATED & PUBLISHED
BY
E-KİTAP PROJESİ & CHEAPEST BOOKS

www.cheapestboooks.com

 **www.facebook.com/EKitapProjesi**

ISBN: 978-625-6308-74-9
Copyright, 2024 by e-Kitap Projesi
Istanbul

Categories: Adventure, Community
Country of Origin: United States
Cover: © Cheapest Books
License: CC-BY-4.0

For full terms of use and attribution, http://creativecommons.org/licenses/by/4.0/

Contributing: Hari Kumar Nair

About the Book

Almost a thousand years ago, an Indian scholar called Hemachandra discovered a fascinating number sequence. A century later, the same sequence caught the attention of Italian mathematician Fibonacci, who wrote about it.

The Fibonacci sequence, as it began to be called, was straightforward enough - what made it fascinating was that this particular set of numbers was repeated many, many times in nature - in flowers, seashells, eggs, seeds, stars... Find out more inside this book!

Numbers. We use them everyday. To count, measure, call friends on the phone and even to find out what something costs. But did you know you can also use numbers to create patterns - geometrical shapes, rangoli designs, and more? Did you know number patterns can be seen within patterns in nature?

But first, what is a 'Number Pattern'?

A Number Pattern is a sequence of numbers where each number is connected to the previous one in ONE specific way.

Take this very simple number pattern: 0, 1, 2, 3, 4. .. How is each number in this sequence connected to the one before it? Well, every number in this sequence is the previous number with 1 ADDED to it. Here's another number pattern: 14 ,12 ,10 ,8, 6. .. Each number in this sequence is the previous number with 2 SUBTRACTED from it.

Now for a slightly more tricky pattern: 0, 1, 3, 6,

10 ,15 ...

How does this sequence work? Let's see.

$$0 + 1 = 1$$

$$1 + 2 = 3$$

$$3 + 3 = 6$$

$$6 + 4 = 10$$

$$10 + 5 = 15$$

Do you see the pattern here? What will the next number in this sequence be?

Yes, 21 ,because $15 + 6 = 21$.

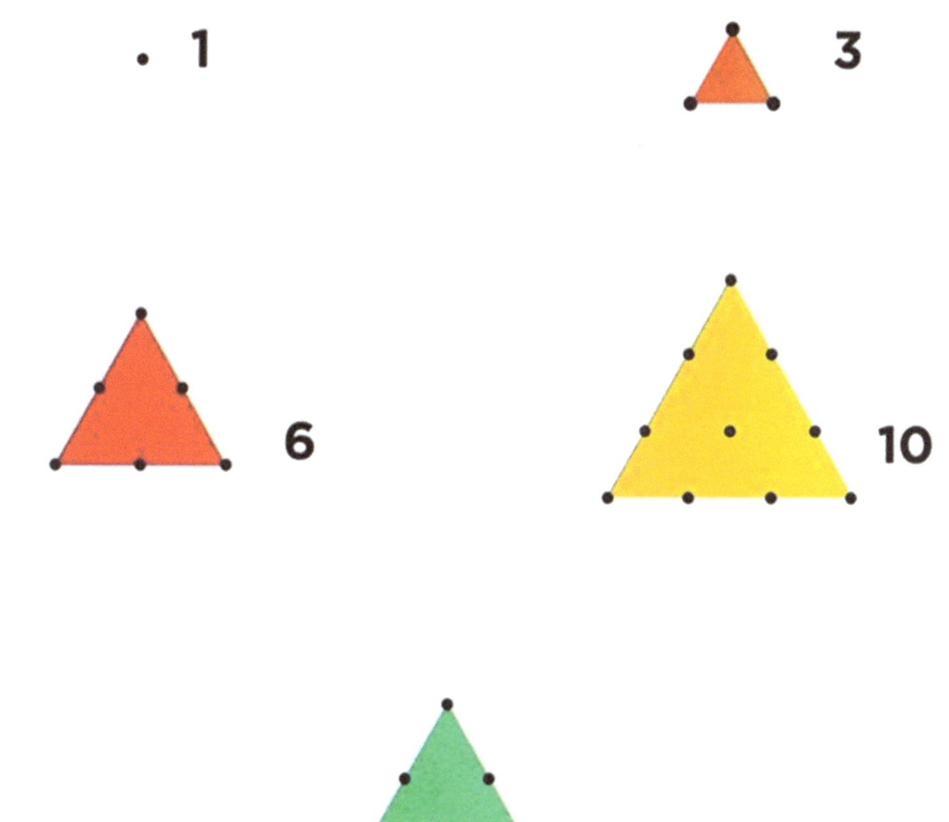

Now, let's take the 'number pattern' we just

discussed: 1, 3, 6, 10 ,15 ... , and see if we can

create a 'SHAPE pattern' from it. We can! We now have a 'shape pattern' of triangles that get bigger and bigger as we increase the number of dots according to our number pattern! A number pattern has become a shape pattern!

If you found that interesting, it's time you were introduced to a beautiful number sequence called the Fibonacci (or Hemachandra) Sequence of numbers.

The Fibonacci Sequence of numbers goes like this:

0, 1, 1, 2, 3, 5, 8, 13 ,21 ,34 ...

Can you find the pattern that connects these numbers? Yes! Every number in the Fibonacci Sequence is the sum of the two numbers before it! Like this.

$$0 + 1 = 1$$

$$1 + 1 = 2$$

$$2 + 1 = 3$$

$$3 + 2 = 5$$

$$5 + 3 = 8$$

$$8 + 5 = 13$$

$$13 + 8 = 21$$

$$21 + 13 = 34$$

Got it? Good. Now for the REALLY interesting part - linking this number pattern to patterns in nature.

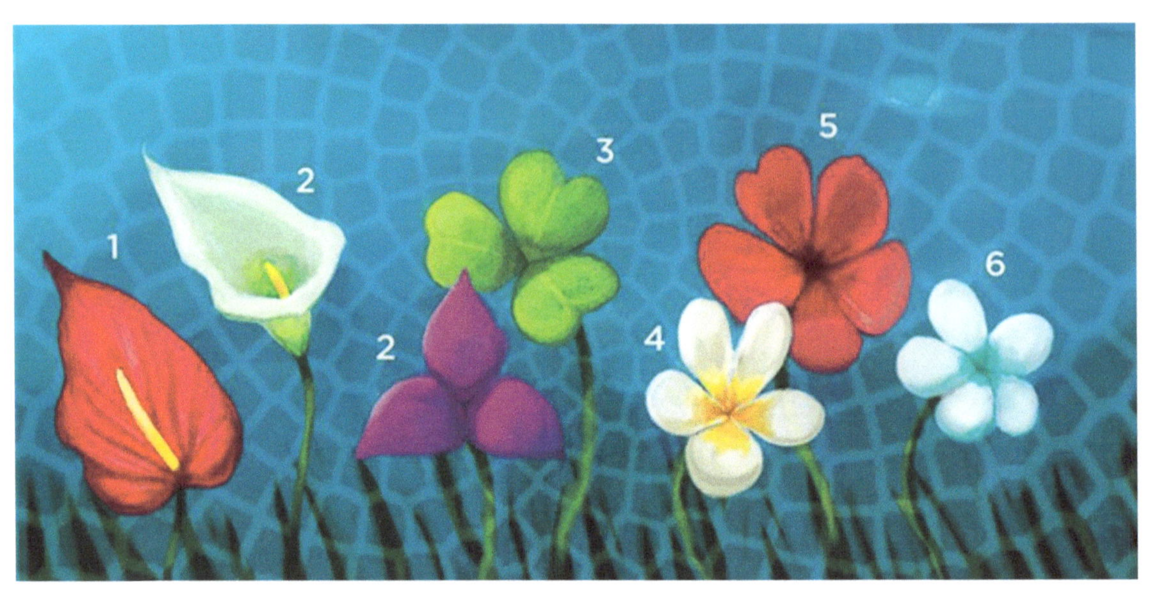

The number of petals flowers have are often linked to Fibonacci numbers! Can you think of flowers with 1, 3 and 5 petals? (These are all Fibonacci numbers.)

Here are some examples to help you along.

1 petal - 1. Anthurium; 2. Calla lilies

3 petals - 2. Bougainvillea; 3. Clovers

5 petals - 4. Temple tree; 5. Hibiscus; 6. Jasmine

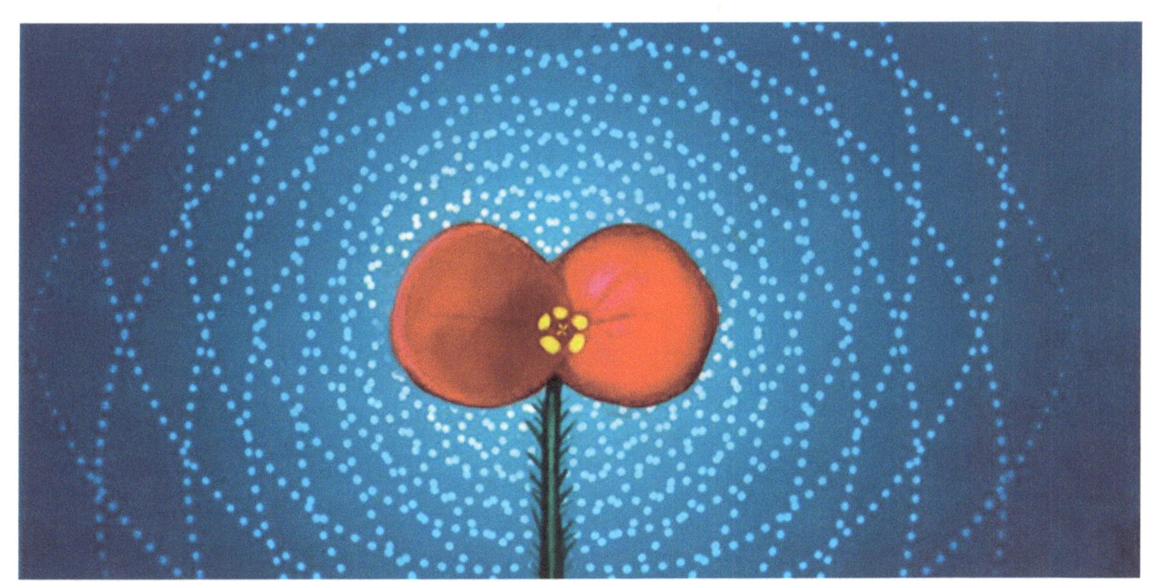

Flowers with 2 petals are not very common. The Crown of Thorns, which you see here, is one example. Flowers with 4 petals (4 is NOT a Fibonacci number) are also rare. Count the petals of flowers that you come across and see for yourself!

The most interesting flower of all, where the Fibonacci sequence is concerned, is the daisy. Different daisy species have 13, 21, or 34 petals - which are all Fibonacci Numbers!

There are even more complex and stunning patterns in nature that appear to be based on the Fibonacci numbers.

If you are willing to do a little math, you can see it for yourself.

Shall we try it out?

Now, what would we get if we squared* each of the numbers in the Fibonacci sequence?

Fibonacci Sequence: 1, 1, 2, 3, 5, 8, 13, etc.

If we 'squared' each of these numbers, we would get:

$1 \times 1 = 1$ Squared or $1^2 = 1$

$2 \times 2 = 2$ Squared or $2^2 = 4$

$3 \times 3 = 3$ Squared or $3^2 = 9$

$5 \times 5 = 5$ Squared or $5^2 = 25$

$8 \times 8 = 8$ Squared or $8^2 = 64$

13 x 13 = 13 Squared or 13 ^2 = 16 9< br/>So the Fibonacci Sequence Squared: 1 - 4 - 9 - 25 - 64 - 16 9- etc.

*When you multiply a number by itself, the number is 'squared'.

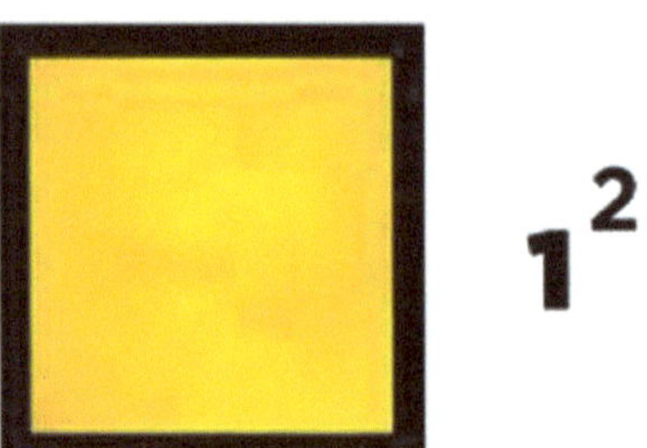

1^2

2^2

Now, just like we converted a number pattern into a shape pattern with the triangles before, let's try to convert the Fibonacci Sequence Squared into a shape pattern. Let's try to DRAW 1^2, 2^2, 3^2 and so on.

1^2 is easy enough - it is just one square.

2^2 is drawn like this - 2 squares across and 2 squares down.

We know that $2^2 = 4$, and there are 4 squares in the figure (we call this figure a 'grid').

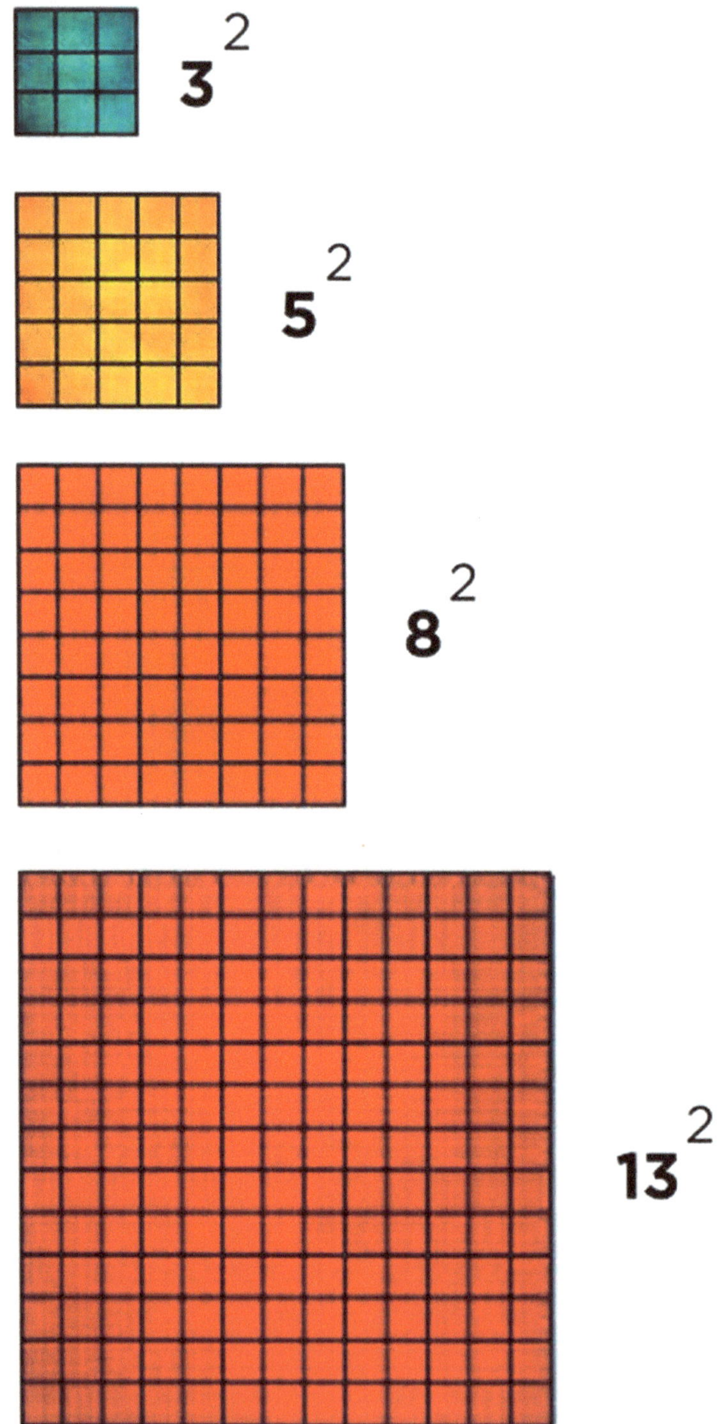

3^2
5^2
8^2
13^2

Similarly, 3^2 is drawn as 3 squares across and 3 squares down. Again, we know that $3^2 = 9$, and there are 9 squares in the grid.

5^2 is drawn as 5 squares across and 5 squares down, making a grid with 25 squares, 8^2 as 8 squares across and 8 squares down, making a grid with 64 squares, 13^2 squared is drawn as a grid with 169 squares, and so on.

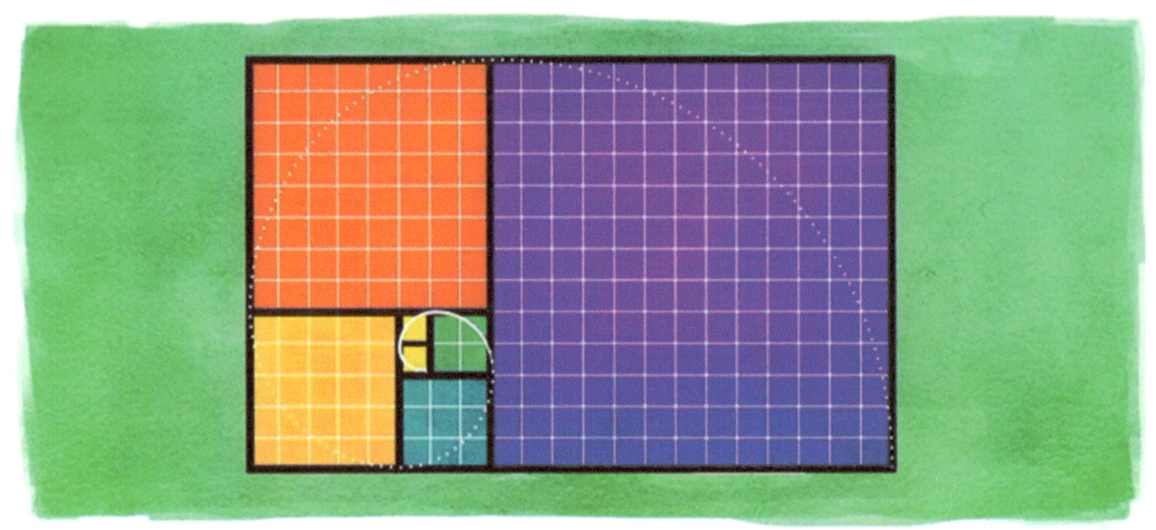

Now, let's push all the grids we've drawn so far towards each other, and arrange them like in the picture.

Done? Now draw a smooth curved line from one corner of the smallest grid to its opposite end, as shown in the figure.

Now take the same curved line through each of the other grids, from smallest to biggest, from corner to opposite corner, ending with the 13 squared grid. What we get is a lovely spiral pattern.

what is the link between this spiral pattern created by squared Fibonacci numbers, and nature? Well, the exact same Fibonacci Spiral can be found in nature! Where? Let's see, shall we?

Here's the Fibonacci Spiral with one more grid -

21 ^2 - added to our original figure.

See how the spiral continues? Does the spiral

look familiar?

Of course it does!

You can see the Fibonacci spiral in seashells (although you might have to twist your head around a bit to see the exact spiral pattern of the previous page)...

... snail shells

... even eggs (see how this spiral goes the other way (anti-clockwise) as compared to the clockwise spiral on page 14 ?)!

Even larger structures like hurricanes and even some galaxies seem to follow the Fibonacci Spiral pattern.

Fascinating, isn't it?

A BRIEF HISTORY

To end this exciting tale of Fibonacci Numbers, let's touch briefly upon the history of the Fibonacci Number Sequence.

In the 11 th century (almost 10 00 years ago), a Jain scholar and monk called Hemachandra, who lived in present-day Gujarat, discovered an interesting mathematical pattern while studying poetry and music. He was looking at the number of different ways in which you could combine 'long' and 'short' sounds in music to create different rhythmic patterns.

Around 10 0y ears later, an Italian mathematician called Leonardo Fibonacci (c.11 70 - c.12 50)- wrote about the very same mathematical pattern in his book Liber Abaci, or 'Book of Calculation' in 12 02 .Fibonacci travelled extensively along the Mediterranean coast, meeting merchants from the East and finding out about how they did mathematics.

It is possible that Fibonacci came across Hemachandra's sequence during his travels, but since he was the first one to introduce it to Europe, these numbers became known to the world as the Fibonacci Sequence.

A word of caution:

Although there are many examples in nature that seem to follow the Fibonacci pattern, there are also many examples in nature that do not - like four leaved clovers, or flowers with 4 petals.

What's intriguing, though, is how often these Fibonacci Numbers do appear in nature. So far, scientists haven't figured out WHY nature seems to love Fibonacci numbers so much.

Maybe YOU can find the answer when you grow up!

End of the Story